If You Met A Yeti...

By Amy Leask
Illustrated by Sheniece Toni Cater

Copyright © Red T Media, 2019.

All rights reserved under International and Pan-American Copyright Conventions. No part of this book may be reproduced or utilized in any form or by any means, electronically or mechanically, including scanning, photographing, photocopying, recording, or by any information storage and retrieval system without permission in writing from the publisher.

International Standard Book Number: 978-1-927425-22-0

Author: Amy Leask
Illustration: Sheniece Toni Cater
Design: Sheniece Toni Cater
Publisher: Ben Zimmer
Editor: Karina Sinclair

"If You Met A Yeti..." first edition published by:
Red T Media,
8560 Tremaine Rd, Second Floor,
Milton, ON, Canada L9T 2X3

www.RedTKids.com

For Ashton, the inspiration for many great ideas.

If you met a yeti

while playing in the snow,

and they asked you about human beings,

what would they need to know?

Would you scratch your head and tell them

humans are a set of parts,

including arms and legs, and hands and feet,

and eyes, and smiles, and hearts?

Each human has a body.

We come in different shapes and sizes.

So many different shades and hues,

these varieties surprise us.

Our bodies help us learn about

the wacky world we live in.

Bodies move and grow, expand, explore

the spaces that we're given.

> Interesting, but is that all?

If you met a yeti

while bopping to the beat,

and they asked about the language

of the humans they might meet,

would you tell them that most humans,

whether they are girls or boys,

like to write and read and move their hands,

and make a lot of noise?

Hai sa dansam!

Pašokime

Our human sounds and human words,
are not just funny squawking.
They are how we share and laugh
with others who are talking.

And if you wander somewhere else,
to places far away,
you will learn some different words that
folks are keen to say.

Allons danser!

Kuja tucheze!

让我们跳舞吧

Ајде да танцуваме

Fascinating! Anything more?

If you met a yeti,

> while waiting for the bus,

> and they asked you what it means to say

> that someone's "one of us",

would you kindly introduce them

> to the person by your side,

> and explain that friends and family

> can fill us up with pride?

A human by itself is fine,

but most times it would seem,

we like to be a group, a bunch,

a posse, or a team.

And with our peeps, we build a home,

a village or a town,

so when we need somebody,

we know others are around.

> Sound cozy. What else you got?

If you met a yeti

while paddling in the lake,

and they asked about the many things

that humans like to make,

would you write a list of all the stuff

with which we like to tinker,

the stuff we build, create, invent

that comes from minds of thinkers?

We make gadgets, gizmos, structures,
things that help us move around,
some things simply nice to look at,
things that make amazing sounds.

We invent so many new things,
it's enough to make you dizzy!
Yes, our human minds and human hands
seem happiest when they're busy.

Wow! You guys **ARE** busy!

If you met a yeti

while picking out a snack,

and they asked you what our minds are like,

how would you answer back?

Would you try to paint a picture

of what lives inside our heads,

what we think about while wide awake,

or dreaming in our beds?

Oh, the things we can imagine,

new ideas come by the tonne!

Humans think of things that aren't yet real,

that haven't yet begun!

We imagine things we'd like to see,

new things we aim to seek.

Imagining is how we find

the ways we are unique.

What nifty minds you have!
Is there anything else?

If you met a yeti

while waiting for the bell,

and they asked you why it is we think

that learning is so swell,

would you tell them that we're keen to teach

each other how to do things,

how we like to spread ideas and thoughts,

and think each other through things?

We teach and learn when we are young
in something called a school,
but it can happen anywhere.
We need to share what's cool!

We learn from friends, from doing work,
from fathers and from mothers,
and while teaching things to someone else,
it's us that we discover.

Ah, I see!

If you met a yeti

watching clouds float through the sky

and they wondered at how human beings

are always asking "why"

would you tell them that the lot of us

with almost no exceptions,

spend our mornings, noons, and evenings

asking many kinds of questions?

We want to know what's right and wrong,
how some things work (or don't),
why this means that, not something else,
how will turns into won't.

We wonder why the sky is blue
and why a frog is green,
and like our yeti friends, we ask
"What makes a human being?"

Bingo!

So if you meet a yeti,

or any other curious creature,

when you've finished telling them YOUR thoughts,

why not make THEM the teacher?

Maybe ask about their yeti life,

the places they have been.

What makes a yeti different

from the humans that they've seen?

Your yeti might explain to you

(as yetis often do)

that when you learn about someone else,

you also learn about

You.

Manufactured by Amazon.ca
Bolton, ON